The Life of Ellie

THE STUFFY ADVENTURES: BOOK 1

Dedication Page

My husband Joel, for working so hard and always giving me the support I need. Everly, for showing me how to see life through the eyes of an angel. Carson, for your beautiful confidence, and for sharing Ellie with the world - you're one of a kind!

And to Becky, my angel-in-law, for all of your wisdom and dedication - Jan

~~~~~~~~~~~~~~~~~~

For my mom, who has supported and encouraged my creativity since I picked up my first crayon. - Nick

On the day Ellie arrived, Carson stood at the window watching deliveries come to his house. Most of the packages were for his new baby sister, Everly.

Usually, the boxes were brown and square, but as Carson watched the mailman grab a large white box from the back of his truck and walk to the front steps, he knew something special was inside.

"Maybe it's a big, green dinosaur!" he thought. "Or an awesome blue shark!" His imagination ran wild.

He was so excited; he couldn't wait to see inside! "Slow down, buddy," Dad said, laughing. "This is for Everly." Dad told Carson to stick his hand in the box and guess what it was. Carson reached in and felt something soft and fuzzy. But what was it? He squeezed and slowly pulled it from the box.

Carson's eyes grew wide and his mouth dropped open. He was holding the most beautiful pink stuffed elephant he'd ever seen. She had big floppy ears, shiny grey eyes, a long pink trunk, and a cute little tail. Carson hugged the elephant around her super puffy neck, and gently whispered "Ellie".

"How wonderful!" said Mom and Dad. "We'll give her to Everly when she's older." And just like that, they closed the box and took it away.

Weeks passed and the box sat on a dusty closet shelf, forgotten. Ellie felt sad and lonely in the dark with no one to play with.

"I'm meant for more than this!" she cried, thinking of the little boy with messy blonde hair and bright blue eyes. But where did he go?

One day, Carson was playing hide-and-seek with Mom and Dad. He squeezed into an upstairs closet and giggled to himself. "They'll never find me here," Carson said. "Ready or not, here we come!" Mom and Dad shouted.

Carson cracked the door open, and from the corner of his eye, saw a white box sitting on the shelf. Squinting in the darkness, Carson could make out the shape of something long and fuzzy hanging from it. Something long, fuzzy and... PINK! "Ellie!" he yipped.

Carson reached as high as he could but even on his tiptoes, Ellie was too far away. He saw a big wooden chest on the floor and had an idea!

Carefully climbing on top of the chest, he reached again. "Almost," he whispered, and with one final stretch, his fingers wrapped around her trunk.

Carson gave her a giant pull and Ellie flew from the box. Down to the floor they went . . . **PLOP!**

Grabbing Ellie and hugging her tightly, he crooned her name softly as she was back in his arms. Finally, where she belonged.

Mom and Dad walked in to find Carson under a giant heap of pink fluff! "This is the best day ever!" Carson squealed! "Mom, you forgot about this elephant! I really want to keep her! She's so soft, and Baby Sister's too small for her!"

They weren't sure Carson should keep Ellie, but there was something sweet about the two of them tangled up.

Then, Mom and Dad smiled and nodded at each other. They silently agreed, Ellie now belonged to Carson.

From then on, Ellie went everywhere with Carson and saw all the things that he did.

She had picnics on blankets while blowing bubbles into the sky, she went on trips to the beach and to the mountains — and once . . .

. . . she even rode on the back of a horse!

One of his favorite things to do with Ellie was to throw her way up into the air and catch her when she came down.

She loved watching the world in action through this little boy's eyes!

One day, Mom had Baby Sister on the floor wrapped in a special blanket called a swaddle. Mom was making silly faces and talking to her in a funny, high-pitched voice. The baby smiled and giggled at her mommy. Wanting to join the fun, Carson grabbed Ellie and swaddled her tight.

With only Ellie's face and trunk peeking out, Carson hid his eyes and popped out, giggling. "Peek-a-boo!" he whispered.

Ellie felt so special and silly being wrapped up like a baby!

After swaddling came a family favorite — time to dance! Mom turned the music on, and they boogied around the house. Carson grabbed Ellie and lifted her above his head. He swung her around and around, letting her long arms and legs flip flop all around them. Ellie had never spun so fast!

When the song ended, they fell to the floor laughing, giddy and dazed! From then on, Ellie joined all the daily dance parties!

At bedtime, Mom read Carson a book. He propped Ellie under his head like a pillow. When the lights went out, they snuggled and chatted about the day. Carson recalled the dance party and giggled when he mentioned how he swaddled Ellie like a baby. Ellie's trunk wrapped around Carson's face and he closed his eyes.

They both drifted off to sleep, excited and anxious about the next day . . .

Today was "stuffed animal day," and Carson was bringing Ellie to school! Carson was so excited to show her off. Ellie had never met any of his friends before. She was a little worried that not everyone would like her, but Carson assured her not to worry — that everyone would love her.

At school, she sat at his desk and joined craft time and storytime. She also met all his friends. They each shook her trunk and said, "Nice to meet you, Ellie!" and Ellie knew they all liked her by their friendly smiles! She loved meeting new friends!

Carson and Ellie continue to enjoy all of their days together, but after so much activity, Ellie has begun to look a little worn. Her puffy neck has lost some stuffing and her pink body is a shade lighter. Lots of holes and tears have been repaired, and Mom has had to sew her tail on a time or two (or ten!).

Like all cuddle stuffies, Ellie gets dirty... but she loves bathtime in the washing machine! Carson sits outside the machine and watches her go around and around, like all the times they danced. When she's finished drying, he loves to pull her from the dryer and hold her like the first time they hugged.

Even with all those repairs and washes, she's still the best cuddle stuffy in the world!

Now that Carson is getting older, Mom and Dad sat him down to talk. "Ellie has been so special to you, and to our family. One day," they tell him, "she'll be excited to meet your kids and share her friendship with them, too!"

Carson understands. Someday soon when he is feeling his bravest, Ellie will go back in the closet. This time though she won't be afraid or lonely. She knows that she will be given to another incredible child with messy hair and loving hugs. And the two of them will begin a whole new set of adventures, together.

The end.

Contact

Write to us!

Do you have an "Ellie"? Tell us about it! What are your favorite things to do together? You could be the inspiration for our next book!

Author contact:
Jan Block | jblock503@gmail.com

 The Life of Ellie
 JanBlockAuthor
 www.JanBlock.me

Illustrator contact:
Nick Reitenour | reitenour.paintings@gmail.com

 Nick Reitenour Paintings, Portraits, and Design
 reitenour.paintings
 www.reitenour.com

Erik Block | erikblock47@gmail.com

Author Page

Jan originally envisioned The Life of Ellie as a family relic: a story based on her son's meaningful relationship with his stuffed elephant, Ellie. As she began to write this story and work with an editor, it occurred to her that every home in the world could relate. At times, special stuffed animals can do more for a child than a parent can. Her hope is to hear about other adventures children have with their special stuffies to inspire a line of books called "The Stuffy Adventures." Born in Ohio and raised in Florida, Jan moved to Oregon in 2013, where she married her husband, Joel, and found a career producing large-scale events for a national business publication. Jan and Joel now live along with their two young children outside the Twin Cities in rural Minnesota.

Nick was born in Virginia and grew up in Minnesota, where he attended the Art Institute of Minnesota, graduating in 2005 with a Bachelor's Degree in Graphic Design. After several years working as a designer, Nick decided to switch gears and pursue his dream of working with kids with special needs. He earned a Master's Degree in Special Education from Liberty University in 2013 and currently works as a middle school Special Education teacher in Elk River, Minnesota. Nick enjoys painting portraits and landscapes, and also performs as a "live painter" at local churches, as well as weddings and corporate events all over the Midwest. Nick lives in Monticello, Minnesota with his beautiful wife Stephanie and his three amazing sons, Dexter, Rowan, and Spencer.

Erik was born and raised in small-town Minnesota and spent 20 years in the Fargo/Moorhead area, where he attended Minnesota State University Moorhead, earning a Bachelor's Degree in English Education and a Master of Fine Arts Degree in Creative Writing. He spent a decade working in post-secondary education as an instructor and administrator and has spent the last five years as owner and operator of Fargo-based entertainment company, Red River Trivia. Erik also works as a freelance editor/writing coach and is the author of one young adult novel, Just Jake. He lives in Las Vegas with his fiancee Holly and her two children, Hailey and Blake.

Book Beneficiary

Partial proceeds support **Friends of the Children**. A national organization that drives generational change by empowering youth who face the greatest obstacles with the support of a salaried, professional mentor (called a "Friend") who stays with each child from kindergarten through high school graduation. No matter what.

Together, we have raised $10,000 since the launch of The Life of Ellie. Thanks to the many supporters like: First Republic Bank, Picture This PDX and Logical Position.

Founder & Chairman, Duncan Campbell:
"I wouldn't wish my childhood on anyone and yet without my experiences, I wouldn't have founded Friends of the Children. I wanted to change just one child's life. Through the power of mentoring relationships, thousands of children across the country now have a Friend."

Chief Executive Officer, Terri Sorensen:
"We are incredibly grateful for Jan and her vision for The Life of Ellie. A book of hope and belonging for every child. Every child deserves a caring adult who believes in and encourages them to develop their special skills and talents and reach their full potential."

Jan:
"I'm honored to name Friends of the Children the book beneficiary. I grew up with a similar story as Duncan Campbell and committed myself to breaking the cycle. My hope with this contribution is to change the narrative for kids who were once like me."

For more information or to donate, please go to *FriendsoftheChildren.org*

Book Reviews

The Life of Ellie is a book about loving and caring for a special stuffy. Ellie is a pink, fluffy, and lovable friend of Carson. This is a story of a sweet friendship between a boy and his pink elephant. The two go on adventures together: horseback riding, picnics, and trips to the beach, and even to school. This friendship helped Carson through tough times, as he grows up. Carson is a very thoughtful boy who loves his sister a bunch!

-Piper Peterson, age 11, Monticello, MN | Young Authors Young Artists winner 2017

'**The Life of Ellie**' is a fun book to read because it's about the love of a boy and a stuffed animal. One of my favorite parts was when Carson and his mom and dad were playing hide-and-seek, and then Carson found Ellie! And I also loved when Carson was using his imagination! I think you will love to read this book!

-Hailey Blevins, age 9, Las Vegas, NV.

The Life of Ellie reminds me of the special stuffy I had when I was a little girl, and still have! I feel like all young kids can relate to this book. I love that Ellie has feelings throughout the story, and you can see how the relationship between her and Carson is very strong. My favorite part is knowing Ellie will always have someone to have a dance party with.

-Kemsiey Weekley, age 11, Matthews, NC.

www.ingramcontent.com/pod-product-compliance
Lightning Source LLC
Chambersburg PA
CBHW061754290426
44108CB00029B/2992